A IS FOR ATTITUDE

AN ALPHABETICAL GUIDE TO THE GOOD LIFE

BETH PARKS, Ed.D.

SIBYL MERRITT™
PUBLISHER

Library of Congress Control Number: 2012922856

Publisher's Cataloging-In-Publication Data
(Prepared by The Donohue Group, Inc.)

Parks, Beth.
  A is for attitude : an alphabetical guide to the good life / Beth Parks.

    p. : col. ill. ; cm.

Includes index.
ISBN-13: 978-0-9824565-0-7
ISBN-10: 0-9824565-0-6

1. Attitude (Psychology) 2. Success. 3. Affirmations. I. Title.

BF632 .P37 2013
153.8/5   2012922856

SIBYL MERRITT™
PUBLISHER

DEDICATION

For my "Big Sis"

Katie McCalmont

ACKNOWLEDGMENTS

My sincere thanks go to Marianne Perlak,
Art Director Emerita, Harvard University Press,
for her encouragement and helpful suggestions.

I also thank Letitia Baldwin, Martha Metzler, and Katie and Don McCalmont
for their thoughtful reviews and recommendations.

CONTENTS

INTRODUCTION

Did you ever wish that someone would hand you a recipe for good and happy living? Here it is, sweet and simple. It's called *A Is for Attitude: An Alphabetical Guide to the Good Life*.

You probably wonder exactly what leads to a good life. You may not be sure why some people thrive, while others appear to live under a cloud of misery and bad luck. The trends for certain individuals often hold true no matter who they are, where they live, how much money they have, or which religion they practice. Some people flourish. Others don't.

You may just be starting out in life and can't seem to get things right. There may be times when you feel so down you think you will never be able to get back up again. Perhaps you failed at a relationship or at something you really wanted to do. Maybe you lost a loved one, your job, your health, your money, your home, or something else that was precious and dear to you. Take heart. When things seem at their absolute worst, *A Is for Attitude* can help you the most.

Perhaps you think you already know all the answers. Yet, even if you believe that true and lasting happiness will eventually be yours, the business of daily living sometimes gets in the way.

As you search for fulfillment, be aware of two subtle traps that can keep you from living your life to its fullest. We'll call them *if only* and *more*. Both can keep you from being completely satisfied with who you are and the things you have.

Quite likely, you already let *if only* keep you from thoroughly enjoying what's happening now. You think, "If only I had . . . , then I'd be happy" or "If only I could . . . , then I'd be happy." Every time you think you have what you want, you start yearning for something else. It never seems to end.

And you likely want *more* of everything: more winning, more money, more power, more possessions, more prestige, more sex appeal, and the list goes on. Getting *more* gives you an initial burst of what you believe is happiness, but it doesn't last for long. You want that rush, that high. As soon as the initial euphoria begins to fade, you start seeking the next *more*. It's like an itch you can't quite scratch.

Sometimes it takes a life-altering event to help you realize what is really important to you. In my case, it was cancer. As my own existence seemed about to end, I took a hard look at my life and the lives of the people around me. It became profoundly clear to me that they and I were wasting precious energy on negative thinking and things that really didn't matter in the long run.

In looking for ways to survive cancer, I began focusing on thoughts and behaviors that would help me build my emotional and physical strength. The concepts I identified and put into practice enabled me to face surgery and chemotherapy with humor and renewed vigor. They also prepared me to cope with the deaths of three dear ones within a few months, a near-fatal car accident, and several other events that would have forced many people to give up.

My approach worked so well for me that others took notice and asked for my secrets. I share the pearls of wisdom I learned in *A Is for Attitude*.

HOW THIS BOOK IS ORGANIZED

The concepts addressed in *A Is for Attitude* are organized alphabetically from A to Z. They lead you to the core of who you are as a human being. Their purpose is to help you dump the negatives in your life and latch on to the solid basics that will help you move forward and thrive.

A Is for Attitude offers wisdom handed down from generations of experience. Each concept is distilled to make it easy to understand and remember. A photograph of a person, animal, place, or thing helps to reinforce and breathe life into each topic. Repetition underscores the ideas and allows each concept to stand on its own.

You may question my choice of concepts or argue that other terms would be more appropriate. Using the 26 alphabet letters to start the words forced me to make some difficult decisions. If you read each page carefully, however, you will likely find your preferred concept folded into one or more of the ones addressed.

You may also wonder why I did not specifically discuss religion in this book. Having visited all seven continents, dozens of countries, and all fifty United States, I am acutely aware of the differences in beliefs. However, the truths put forth in *A Is for Attitude* tend to be universally accepted by people of all religions and belief systems around the globe.

The clear, straightforward style of *A Is for Attitude* makes it a useful guide and reference source for everyone from teens to the elderly. It also provides a solid basis for discussions between and among individuals, families, educators, groups, organizations, and societies.

Whatever your age, experience or background, *A Is for Attitude* will help you discover the power within you. Use that power to build a good and happy life.

Enjoy, and live well.

6

ATTITUDE

The secret to leading a healthier, fulfilling and more successful life is staring back at you from your own mirror: your attitude. Attitude, attitude, attitude! How fitting that it begins with the letter A, the first letter of the alphabet.

To understand the importance of attitude, just look at the people around you. Do you prefer those who take a positive, can-do approach to life, or those who put a negative spin on everything? Those who try to do the best possible job, or those who constantly grumble and make excuses for not trying? Those who encourage others to succeed, or those who constantly find fault?

Observe. Let your preferences for other people's attitudes guide your own.

Your attitude determines how you see the world and how others in your life see you. Take a hard, honest look at yourself. Does your attitude help you succeed? If not, and your life seems filled with barriers and bad luck, then it's time to change.

Before you can change your attitude, however, you need to recognize the negatives that assault your thinking and drain your enthusiasm. Headline news is usually bad. Evaluations underscore what you do wrong. Gossip delights in tarnishing your reputation. Religions may claim that you are inherently sinful. Pessimism clouds the air and obscures your view of what is possible and good.

Focus on the positives you want from life and refuse to let the negatives contaminate your thinking. You won't be able to control all the things that happen to you, but you can master how you let those things affect your spirit. Show gratitude for constructive criticism. Apologize for your mistakes. Ask how you can right your wrongs. Don't whine.

Start each day with a smile. Decide what you want to accomplish. Open your mind to fresh opportunities. Stand tall and give a thumbs-up salute as you say over and over, "I can! I can!"

Couple your positive attitude with your abilities, and go out and do your best.

BELIEVE

Next to a positive attitude, your greatest asset is to believe in yourself. If you firmly believe you can do something, you stand a good chance of succeeding. If you believe you will fail, you probably will. You tend to influence your own outcomes.

Quite simply, your brain accepts what you tell it. It does not distinguish between reality and what you believe to be the truth. Feed positive thoughts to your brain and it will likely respond in a positive way. Tell yourself you can't do something and you will probably set yourself up to fall flat.

Start by dropping the "t" off can't. You may find yourself wondering, "What ever made me think I could do this?" Self-doubt is perfectly normal. But when you feel frightened, discouraged or unsure, refuse to give up. Surround yourself with people who will encourage you and cheer you on to greater success.

Ignore those individuals who tell you that something is impossible. You are your own worst enemy if you allow their expectations to limit what you attempt. There is no disgrace in failing to reach the goals you set for yourself. The only shame comes from being too timid to take a chance. The key to reaching your goals is to keep on trying.

Perhaps you have convinced yourself that you can't compete with people you perceive to be smarter, faster, stronger, or somehow better prepared than you. Dump your doubts. Have faith, and work toward your goals without reservation. Success eventually comes to those who believe strongly enough to persevere.

What if you believe in yourself with all your heart and then fail anyway? Setbacks offer valuable lessons that can help you improve. Learn from your mistakes. Recognize the powers that guide you, and move forward.

You can test your wings a thousand times and never get off the ground. Just remember that it only takes one success to start flying.

Believe with all your heart that you can soar to new heights, and you will.

10

CHOICES

Most things in life involve choices. You start choosing as soon as you begin to think.

As a child you choose the foods you like to eat and the games you want to play. As you grow older, your choices become far more complex. You choose what career to pursue, if or whom to marry, where and how to live, and the ways you care for your body.

One choice leads to another in a seemingly endless chain. Good choices tend to lead to other good choices. Bad choices may lead to other bad ones if you don't learn from your mistakes. Try to anticipate the outcomes of your behaviors and adjust your choices accordingly.

You sometimes hear people say, "I had no choice." Wrong. You always have a choice, even if it is not one that you or others prefer. Even doing nothing is a choice.

How you choose determines your destiny. You choose your values and your friends. You choose which doors to open and which to close. You choose if, when and how to communicate. You choose which tasks to undertake, and whether or not to complete those tasks. You choose to accept the status quo or to seek change. You choose a lifestyle that ultimately affects your health, wealth and overall success.

Your philosophy reflects the choices you make as you move through life. You demonstrate your personal philosophy every time you act. You may not even be aware of your choices once your actions have become habits.

How you view your choices reflects your attitude. It is normal to make errors, so view them as educational experiences. Learn from them, and do your best to improve.

The choices you make impact not just you, but also others affected by your actions. You are responsible for the outcomes of your own choices and decisions. If you choose poorly, you may or may not have the freedom to reconsider and choose again.

Be prepared. Think things through before you act, and choose wisely.

DREAM

What did you dream of doing or becoming when you were young? Did your dreams come true? If not, why did your splendid visions and bright hopes slip away?

Dreams that escape the first time still swim around, waiting to be caught again. They lurk just beneath the surface of your imagination, plump with potential and promise, waiting for you to net them.

A dream without action will always remain a dream, but a dream coupled with poorly considered actions might well become a nightmare. Before you act, try to be sure what you want is right not just for you, but also the others your actions will affect.

You must set clear goals if you want to make your dreams come true. The goals must be yours and not someone else's. It does not matter how remote your objectives appear or how impossible they seem to attain. If you know what you want and can see it clearly in your mind, you can likely make it happen. Design a sound and concrete plan so you know precisely where you are heading and how you will get there. Plan your work and work your plan.

If you are to triumph, you need three more things: the patience to tolerate setbacks, the courage to forge ahead, and the passion to complete your tasks. You may not attain your goals exactly when you wish, but life is not always easy or fair. In the end, the tragedy lies not in failing to realize your dreams, but in never having dreams to realize.

Only you can catch your dreams. You might try to blame past failures on various circumstances and other people, but the final responsibility for success rests with you. Forget the past. Concentrate on the possibilities that lie ahead.

Not everyone will understand precisely what you seek or why. Let the naysayers drift on by. They can neither capture nor kill your precious dreams without your consent. It is never too late to revive an old vision or launch a new one.

Aspire to succeed. Cast your net, and turn your dreams into reality.

EXPLORE

Every dream requires a certain amount of exploration if you are to achieve it. Dare to transcend your known boundaries. Set out to discover what you can do.

Exploration calls for both risk and effort. What fears have held you back, and why have you allowed them to limit you? Have you set your own borders and limits, or have you allowed someone else to determine just how far you can go?

Allowing other people to control your frontiers may be easy and convenient, but it restricts you to their horizons and confines your dreams to theirs. Their personal concerns and jealousies may even lead them to block your progress. Have faith in yourself. Resist the urge to let other people's biases, fears and philosophies hem you in.

Every exploration starts with knowing where you are now and where you want to go. Reaching your destination means planning, setting goals, understanding the steps involved, and heading off in the right direction.

You also need to know how to navigate pitfalls and determine when you've gone off course. Be prepared to alter your methods and routes whenever things go awry. Always stick to the moral and ethical high ground so that your conscience will remain clear.

Seek the courage within yourself to explore new thoughts and ideas. Embrace your ambitions. Acquire the knowledge and skills you need to become competent in your chosen tasks.

Discipline yourself to explore the possible. You will make mistakes, but they will be your own. Learn from your errors, and aspire to move forward and upward. Use the proficiency that comes from experience to guide you toward the victories you seek.

All the great explorers took huge chances, and we know them by their legendary accomplishments. If they hadn't tried, we wouldn't even know their names.

Your time is now. Explore!

FORGIVE

If someone hurt you, heal yourself. Begin the process by forgiving.

At the center of most lingering hurts, like a grain of sand that prods an oyster to form a protective pearl, lies at least one painful and irritating memory. It may be so deeply embedded that you have almost forgotten it exists. But there it skulks in the darkness, festering and smoldering, generating layer after irksome layer that rubs against your soul.

Try to identify every hurt and slice through the scars that have built up around it. Pry it apart and see what lies within. Is it a word spoken in anger, or a desertion or betrayal? Is it something that bruised your feelings or eroded your self-esteem?

Healing comes from forgiving, and forgiving takes time, energy and practice. Although you can never change the past, you can modify potential outcomes by changing your behavior now.

The person who hurt you may be shocked to learn that some long-forgotten word or action caused you so much pain. It is not the hurt itself that leads to permanent damage, but your own negative emotions. They can poison your entire outlook or even make you mentally and physically ill.

Try to contact the one who hurt you. If possible, meet and discuss the issue. Leave blame and accusations outside the door. Learn how the other person views the situation and then work together to resolve the problem. An impartial mediator may be able to facilitate the process if your communications start to break down.

Bitterness, ill will and resentment can eat you alive. Stop stewing in your own juices, and use them in a positive way to douse the fires of your misery and despair. Once the fire is extinguished, start rebuilding your relationship. Show genuine interest. Try your best to be humble, sincere and kind.

Sometimes, as unfair as it seems, you will be unable to resolve the issues to your satisfaction. The best thing you can do for yourself is to forgive, let go and move on.

GOLDEN RULE

"Do unto others as you would have others do unto you." The Golden Rule and similar versions prompt you to imagine yourself in someone else's place and act in a way you would like to be treated under the same circumstances.

Most of the world's major religions endorse this reciprocity. At its moral and ethical best, the Golden Rule requires you to understand and look beyond such differences as race, religion, culture, position, nation, personal preferences, and even species. It asks you not to impose your beliefs or actions on others if you do not want them to impose their beliefs or actions on you. It tells you not to scorn if you would not like to be scorned, and to listen if you want to be heard.

Do you want to make a profit regardless of who gets hurt, but would be angry if others profited by hurting you? Do you goof off at your job, but would be annoyed if you were an employer whose workers failed to give you an honest day's work in return for their pay? Would you like to bomb others whose beliefs and policies you dislike, but would be indignant and furious if they dropped bombs on you and your loved ones because they disagreed with you or your country's views? Always consider both sides.

People twist the Golden Rule to say, "He who has the gold makes the rules." We often tolerate bad conduct by those who hold power, but anyone can behave badly. Decide what you will accept and how you will proceed when someone crosses the line.

Individuals everywhere engage in such wrongful acts as lying, cheating, stealing, gossiping, controlling, bullying, manipulating, and making fun of others. If you engage in such hurtful behaviors, would you still act in the same way if you knew you would be on the receiving end?

Now that we have become a global community, we interact in ways we could not have foreseen just a few short years ago. Our conduct affects not just us, but others around the world. We need a consistent standard by which to guide our behaviors if we are to coexist and survive on this small planet.

Live by the Golden Rule, and try to do no harm.

HAPPINESS

Happiness seems like such a simple thing. Why, then, is it so hard to achieve?

Perhaps you think you would finally be happy if only you could do "this" or have "that." Such things may bring you temporary pleasure, but you will always go on to chase another "this" or "that" throughout your life. Lasting gratification will elude you.

Things that stimulate your senses tend to be superficial and fleeting. You may enjoy them at the time, but you will never be satisfied for long.

Other people may tell you the things you need to do to be happy, but what works for them may not be the best for you. You will never find contentment if you are trapped inside a box constructed of someone else's expectations. Know yourself, and be true to who you are.

Happiness often leads to success, but success cannot buy you enduring happiness. Success can be an alluring temptress that both entices and bewitches you. It can also drag you to the depths and turn your heart to stone. Beware the tempting trap.

If you travel to poverty-stricken areas, you may believe that the people who live there are not happy because they live simply and possess so few things. Your assumptions would likely be wrong. Some of the happiest people you will ever meet possess little material wealth. Their happiness comes from within themselves.

Acquiring fancy possessions, holding high positions and amassing lots of money may make you feel good, but such things will not fetch you genuine happiness. They may even become golden prisons that limit your freedom and turn you into a slave.

What will bring you inner happiness? Only you can know for sure. You might seek such things as security, personal achievement, knowledge, someone to love, giving to others, or spiritual awakening. You can't escape the problems of daily living, but there is always joy to be found in your life. Always. You simply need to look for it and let it in.

You've got one life to live. Choose to be happy now.

INVEST

Are you looking for a pot of gold at the end of a rainbow? Forget it. Invest.

Invest is a word you probably hear daily. It makes you think of money: earning it, spending it, winning it, losing it, saving it, inheriting it, and maybe more.

Although material wealth should not be your top priority, try not to be a burden to others. Think of the resources you will need to live comfortably as you age.

Never underestimate the value of investing wisely. Deduct dollars from your paycheck before you ever see them. Invest in financial instruments that will bring you relatively safe and reasonable returns.

Forget the lottery. Your chances of winning big are slim, and few people recoup what they spend on tickets. As the saying goes, a lottery is a tax on people who are poor at math. And forget the get-rich-quick schemes. They may make money for the people who foist them on you, but their clever promises will often leave you holding an empty bag.

If you are looking for the highest return on your investment, invest in yourself. Start by listing your interests, talents and the things you enjoy. Select an occupation that capitalizes on your passions and offers products or services that people are willing to buy. Gain the skills you need to succeed, even if you cringe at the time and money needed to develop your expertise. Know that the harder you work, the luckier you will become.

Investing in your future generates the best returns over the long term. Seeking the highest returns also demands the most patience and risk. You will grow older whether you take action or not, so make the best use of your productive years.

As with any venture, some strategies will appeal to you more than others. Stick with the ones you find comfortable. Ignore the people who try to convince you to switch, and draw extra dividends in satisfaction. Make a living by doing what you truly love.

Invest sensibly in yourself. Have faith in your abilities, and reap your earned rewards.

JOURNEY

Life is a journey, a network of roads that takes you through life. Some roads are selected for you. Others, you choose.

You often pick highways that lead you to specific destinations, expecting that each will bring you fulfillment. I'll be happy when I . . . graduate . . . get my own place . . . find the right job . . . go where I want . . . live where I wish . . . get promoted . . . marry . . . see the kids off on their own . . . have money for the things I want to buy or do . . . be recognized for my achievements . . . .

The list goes on, but no specific end point seems to satisfy you for very long. Cherish the unexpected side trips that happen along the way. You may never follow the same route twice, so take time to notice and enjoy the things around you as you pass.

Life's journey can take you over some extremely rough roads. Expect bumps, construction, frost heaves, potholes, accidents, speed traps, dead ends, and anything else that can aggravate you and slow you down. But setbacks can be good. They shock you out of complacency, and they help you to appreciate the smoother parts of your trip.

You may resent the inevitable delays, but a re-route can often result in unexpected pleasures. It is the detour that takes you to the dirt road time forgot, the fertile valley where you can see both ends of a glorious rainbow at the same time, and the mountaintop that affords you spectacular views of the countryside below.

Sometimes the road of life seems more like a conveyor belt than a causeway. It moves you in one direction, forward in time. People hop on and off, and some fall by the wayside.

You may ride the belt passively, neither knowing nor caring where it is taking you. Perhaps you know its destination, but you fear what lies ahead.

You can often control where you go in life if you know where you want to end up and how you're going to get there. Draw a map, pack your bags and enjoy your journey.

KNOWLEDGE

Man assigned himself the scientific name *Homo sapiens sapiens*. These Latin words translate as "man wise wise," or "man the very, very wise." Are we as bright as we claim, or does the scientific name merely reflect our species' arrogance?

We refer to owls as wise, but wisdom implies both knowledge and understanding. Both must be used together to achieve morally and ethically acceptable results.

Do not confuse wisdom with intelligence. A person who scores poorly on an intelligence test may make wise decisions with wonderful outcomes. Conversely, a person who gets a high score on the same test can make poor decisions that cause great pain.

We humans tend to focus on today rather than all the tomorrows to come. We treat symptoms rather than prevent disease. We wage war rather than work together to solve problems. We place a higher value on politics, profits and unlimited growth than on the long-term impacts we have on our planet. Should we consider such actions wise?

Our world consists of interdependent parts connected much as the strands of a spider's web. A tug on one strand transmits vibrations across the entire network. Today, the failure of a large company sends shock waves through the global economy. Pollutants from factories travel on the wind across the land and oceans to poison someone else's air and water. The extinction of one species impacts others that rely upon it to survive.

Begin to understand your role in the world by getting to know yourself. Recognize and analyze what prompts you to think and behave as you do.

Although you may believe you are an individual acting alone, you are actually part of a much greater whole. Almost everything you say or do has an impact on someone or something else. Impacts radiate out from you in concentric circles to the larger world in which you live. Try to understand the potential aftermaths of your decisions and actions.

Use your knowledge and common sense to make good decisions. And know that all your decisions, wise or not, will endure as your legacy after you're gone.

LOVE

Love is a word we use day in and day out. The term rolls off our tongues without much thought on our part, and we rarely stop to think about what it really means.

Love is not merely a strong affection. It is a medley of powerful emotions that you experience in different ways. You may channel it toward such entities as persons, places, things, sensations, ideas, ideologies, the divine, and even yourself.

Although you may initially think of "being in love," your love for others runs across a broad spectrum of attachments. It may range from lust to romance, from passion to compassion, and from friendships to long-term commitment and support.

At its purest, love means placing the needs of others above your own. If you have never thought of it this way, try it now. Make a list of all the people whose needs and welfare you would place above your own for an extended period of time. Of those you listed, for how many would you willingly lay down your life? Does that number surprise you?

Merely loving is not enough. Seek to love unconditionally. Unconditional love means accepting others as they are with no goal of changing them into what you would like them to be. It requires you to appreciate and tolerate others as you would have them appreciate and tolerate you, despite your differences.

Love is selfless. It cannot be bought or sold. It means forgiving, even when forgiving seems unwarranted or unfair. Love expects nothing in return. If payback is a cornerstone of what you feel, then what you feel is something less than love.

The wonderful thing about love is that it is infinite. The more you give, the more you have to give. And the more you give, the more you ultimately receive. The love you give eventually returns, often from a different or unexpected source.

In your final hours, it will not be the money you made or where you lived or the car you drove that will have brought you true happiness. It will be the love you gave and the lasting good that came from that love.

MOTIVATION

You can gaze at some far-off destination and dream of arriving, but dreaming alone will never get you there. You need to motivate yourself if you want to stand in that distant spot. You must determine where you want to go and commit to making the trip. You must then choose how you will travel, how you will pay for it, and what you will need when you arrive. Finally, you need to start moving. Going somewhere doesn't mean just to a place. It can be whatever you want to accomplish in your lifetime.

Deciding to make an excursion may be the most difficult portion of the process for you. You may think about it. You may talk about it. You may say, "Someday, I'd like to . . . . ," but you never get around to taking that first step.

And then come such inevitable excuses as "I don't have time" or "It costs too much." Your excuses will probably boil down to a list of things you don't want to admit to others or even to yourself. Typical cop-outs include "I'm afraid," "I'm not smart enough," "I don't know where or how to get help," "I don't want to ask," "I don't want to take the risk," and "I don't want to put out the effort."

It is easy to grow complacent in days filled with routines and low expectations. You may feel as if you will live forever, and there is no big rush to do things now. But life has a way of sneaking up behind you and then passing you by. Your inaction and excuses will slowly rob you of your potential, and time will eventually run out.

Stop procrastinating. Jolt yourself into action. If you have been patiently waiting for "someday" to arrive, just say, "That someday is today." Set a concrete deadline to achieve each goal. Stick to your plan as if your life depends on it. It does.

When your days on earth are over and you look back over your life, what will you have accomplished? Will your achievements have reflected your hopes, abilities and ideals? Will they have made you proud? What will you wish you had done, or wish you hadn't?

If you still have things you want to do, start doing them now before you lose the chance. Motivate yourself, and reach your destination while you still can.

NATURE

We live on a planet we call Earth. As far as we can prove to date, Earth is the only planet in our universe that supports life as we know it. Let's define life and all Earth's natural phenomena as "nature."

An ecosystem in nature consists of a complex environmental unit in which such things as plants, animals and microorganisms function in balance with such non-living things as soil, water and the atmosphere. Earth is called a "closed" ecosystem because it has the capacity to sustain itself without human intervention.

You create a portion of an ecosystem whenever you construct a terrarium or aquarium. These are called "open" systems because they require you to add water and food, as well as remove waste, to keep them in balance. You must also maintain the proper levels of light, gases and temperature if your creations are to survive.

A terrarium or aquarium is called a vivarium, or place of life. The nice thing about a small vivarium is that you can quickly see when it is in trouble. Once you have identified a problem, you can often correct it easily and at a reasonable cost.

The trouble with the big vivarium we call Earth is that it is difficult to see where imbalances lie, let alone repair them. Scientists try to identify and report dilemmas, but some people deny that problems exist. Others flatly refuse to acknowledge any data that threaten their special interests or potential profits.

Even if you could get people to agree on the issues and what needs to be done, few would want to take responsibility or pay for remedial actions. Some would rather abandon Earth and devote their energy to seeking other planets to colonize and exploit.

What we do today and tomorrow will affect the balance of nature a hundred, a thousand or even a million years from now. We all need to work together and hold each other accountable for our actions.

Think before you act. Consider the greater good of our planet, and act responsibly.

OPPORTUNITY

Opportunities don't usually knock. You have to go looking for them. They like to disguise themselves, so your challenge is to recognize a good one when you see it.

An opportunity may look so scary at first that you don't dare take a chance on it. It asks you to jump from a secure, known place to something entirely new. The gap between the known and the unknown may seem so wide that bridging it requires a leap of faith.

While opportunities drift all around you, they may not call attention to themselves. Don't be afraid to ask for identification. If the big ones rebuff you, just reach out and grab a handful of smaller ones. They may not look like much, but you can use them as stepping stones to build a respectable path to your success.

An opportunity may turn you off by its drab appearance or unpleasant manner. If you ignore it in favor of chasing rainbows, however, it may quickly disappear. Once it's gone, there is little chance that you will ever see it again.

Obstacles and problems are merely opportunities draped with nettles. You may be tempted to avoid them to keep from being stung. If you handle them carefully, though, you stand to reap valuable rewards.

Some of the most formidable opportunities offer the best and most lasting benefits. Prepare well. Have the courage to reach out and embrace them as you move forward.

Look back over the course of your life. What opportunities did you pass up that had been there for the taking? What stopped you? What did you ultimately lose?

Your attitude often determines which opportunities you select and how you treat them after they're yours. You may pick a poor one, but don't despair. Every mistake offers an opportunity to learn from your experience. Instead of giving up, try again. Each day offers you fresh opportunities. Missing one doesn't take you out of the game.

Know what you want, and recognize your abilities. Be ready to snag a good opportunity whenever one comes your way.

PLAY

Adults seem to have an unwritten rule that they should shun play and devote their efforts toward work and the business of living. The sooner you realize that work and play are not mutually exclusive, the sooner you will recognize that both types of behaviors are equally important to a happy, balanced life.

Too many people sacrifice their ideals in return for money and security. Year after year they work at jobs they despise. They spend much of their time impatiently waiting for days off, anticipating vacations, and looking forward to the time when they can retire. Fun gets shoved under the table, and latent pleasures wither and die.

We tend to get so bound up in work that we ignore the wonderful people and things around us. We refuse to get silly. We neglect to laugh. We bind ourselves in drudgery. We forget that we have the power to break our restricting chains.

When fun sneaks up on us, we throw a blanket over it and pretend it isn't there.

If your work doesn't include fun, then you are probably going about it the wrong way. There should be more to work than just seeking such ends as monetary rewards, power or prestige. If you are not having a good time, reconsider your priorities.

Work changes into play when you have the ability to act freely. Your motivation and direction comes from within. When you feel empowered to imagine, explore and invent, you can create the most amazing things and ideas. Laughter comes easily and often, and learning assumes an aura of joy.

Play doesn't mean goofing off, however. It can have both purpose and a serious edge. Coupled with fun, it also fosters cooperation and a sense of belonging. Growing old doesn't mean having to give up either play or fun, but losing them may make you feel older than you are. Nourish them to slow your aging process.

Play and fun outperform many medicines in keeping you healthy. Enjoy a daily dose.

QUESTION

You may have heard the myth that lemmings will blindly follow each other until they plunge off a cliff to their deaths. The story serves as a metaphor for people who fail to question their own beliefs or actions. They steadfastly follow their leaders, even when those leaders take them down dangerous or potentially fatal paths.

The lemming metaphor is right on target. Most of us live our daily lives through habit. We rarely consider how or why we acquired our beliefs and behavioral patterns. We ignore the consequences they invite, and we seldom challenge conventional wisdom. We tend to go along with regional or cultural norms. We resist raising issues that may bring criticism raining down upon us. We conform.

Do you believe that you are the exception to the lemming rule? Stop and think about how you live your life. Is your religion the same as that of your parents? Do you always accept what you were taught in school? Do you belong to the same political party as your relatives and neighbors? Do you question political actions when the party in power is yours?

A few centuries ago, everyone "knew" the earth was both flat and the center of the universe. People who questioned such assumptions were roundly scorned. Some were even accused of heresy and either severely punished or killed.

Things have changed little over time. People still find themselves being ridiculed or condemned when they challenge popular opinions about such things as religious beliefs or actions, blind allegiance to a flag, or a country's economic and military policies.

Raising questions about society's norms is tough and requires courage. It takes us out of what is passive and safe, and places us squarely on the firing line. But when we don't raise questions, we shackle ourselves to the status quo. We shirk responsibility. We allow bad things to happen. We turn a collective blind eye, either hoping that change will somehow occur, or that someone else will lead the way to enlightenment.

Don't be afraid to ask questions. Take pride in your integrity. If you discover the truth, speak out. Be bold and stand your ground, even if you stand as one against the many.

RESPONSIBILITY

"It's not my fault!"

Does it seem to you that those who do something wrong or make mistakes are quick to shift the blame? It is always the fault of (fill in the blank) . . . parents . . . schools . . . the media . . . video games . . . society . . . the government . . . the system . . . .

Hogwash! You are solely responsible for your own behaviors. Regardless of the influences upon you, you are the one who ultimately chooses to behave in a certain way. Your actions lead to consequences, and those consequences are yours to bear.

If you behave badly, you always have the power to change. Stop making excuses. Instead of saying, "It didn't get finished," say "I didn't finish it." Instead of saying, "The car went out of control," say "I lost control of the car."

Your responsibilities extend beyond your words and actions to include the things you failed to say or do. Standing by idly and watching others do wrong is just as bad and dangerous as if you did the wrong thing yourself.

You always have choices. If you make the best choices you can, given the best information you can obtain at the time, you will have little to regret. You still need to take responsibility for the consequences of your choices. You must be accountable for how your decisions affect yourself and others, both now and for the years to come.

You make a common mistake if you shelter other people and absolve them of the responsibility for their actions. You simply enable them to continue behaving badly. If they don't learn, someone else will suffer or have to shoulder the burdens they impose.

Above all else, be a responsible ancestor. Bring children into this world only if you can afford to feed, clothe and educate them. They and their descendants will ultimately be responsible for the world they inherit. They will pass their impacts along to future generations, as well as to our planet.

Accept responsibility, and teach your children to accept theirs.

SMILE

Never underestimate the power of a smile. No matter where you go in this world, it is the one thing that everyone recognizes and appreciates. It radiates warmth and welcome, and it cuts across such potential barriers as language, customs, ideologies, and doctrines.

A smile costs you nothing. However, it makes a down payment on happiness, harmony and peace. The flash of a smile can pick a person up from the darkest depths and cast a pleasing glow over the dreariest surroundings. A smile can serve as potent medicine to treat an aching soul.

In those dreadful times when you seem to be facing endless days and nights with nothing but pain and despair, smile as if you mean it. Conjure up at least one pleasant memory to fuel the broadest possible grin. Once you see how much better you feel, practice smiling over and over again until it becomes a joyful habit.

Smile's cousin, humor, is another powerful ally to help you navigate life's many traps and pitfalls. The best humor is neither cruel nor targets someone else. It is the kind you use to poke fun at yourself, and it is perhaps the most humanizing gesture of all. It invites others not to loathe or make fun of you, but to admire your humility, forthrightness and courage.

Smile's fraternal twin, laughter, helps you to enjoy life even more. At its best it is outright and uncontrolled, a real tummy tickler that makes you forget your challenges, heartaches and troubles. Laughter is infectious, but don't waste your time seeking an antidote. Spread it to others until it becomes an outright epidemic.

Smile, humor and laughter skip hand in hand through our lives. You may be tempted to slam the door in their shiny faces when you're feeling miserable or downhearted, but the cheery little trio can turn a gloomy existence into a joyous one. You simply need to invite them in.

Turn the wrinkles of your frown upside down. Smile.

TIME

"I don't have time."

We all say it. We all mean it. But what we often forget is that each one of us gets the same amount of time, 24 hours or 1440 minutes, in each full day of our lives. What we do with our time determines who we are.

The most successful and famous people of this or any other period in history had the same number of minutes in every day as everyone else. The difference between them and the rest of us lay in how they chose to spend their time.

We talk about spending time, wasting time, killing time, waiting for the time, wishing for more time, saving time, making time, having time on our hands, and even doing time. We make it sound as if we can manipulate time. We can't. What we can do is use each moment wisely to accomplish what we want while we are alive.

You likely have the time you need to do many of the things you wish. What you may lack is the will. Only you can determine what you want to do with the time you have, and only you can know if your efforts are genuine, wise and efficient.

Of all your possessions, time is by far the most important. You may not recognize its value until time has run out. If you knew you would die tomorrow, what would you trade for just one more day or one more year? What would you choose to do with the added minutes and hours?

The best gift you can give yourself is to spend your time doing the things you love. The happiest people among us are those who thoroughly enjoy the things they do every day, including their work. If you don't love your work, consider changing careers.

When you spend even a single moment regretting the things you did not do with the time you were given, you have effectively wasted that precious moment. Most people want to grow old, but the quality of time you have left is far more important than its quantity.

Make the best of every minute. When time is gone, it's gone for good.

UNKNOWN

Do you fear the unknown? Do you let that fear determine how you live your life? If so, then it's time to drop kick your anxieties into the stratosphere.

Fear is a four-letter word. It is potentially your greatest enemy. It can prevent you from seeking new experiences, exploring your options and pursuing your dreams.

Which do you fear more, the unknowns of life or the unknowns of death? You may say death, but it is usually the fear of life that keeps you from doing the things you want.

In life, you face unknowns when you consider going off to school, taking a new job, investing your money, making a speech, visiting new places, or doing anything you haven't done before. You may find yourself paralyzed by fear of criticism, failure, or somehow getting hurt. But if you don't act, you let all the potential rewards pass you by.

Fear is the bogeyman hiding under your bed of rationality. It is the demon that defeats you because you fail to kill it with reason.

Fear is a sickness you can overcome. Heal yourself by deciding to act. List the possible outcomes that frighten you. Learn all you can about each situation so you can prepare for it, and do bits and pieces of the things you fear the most. Even the smallest successes will boost your confidence and help to build your courage.

As you become aware of your own mortality, you face another set of fears. You will likely worry about pain and suffering, being alone, and getting adequate physical and emotional support. You may also agonize over finances, religious beliefs and the issues faced by your loved ones.

Death may be your greatest unknown, so take a moment to put it into perspective. All living things eventually die. Dying is a part of life, and it is every bit as natural as being born. The less you fear death, the less you will fear life.

Sail into the unknowns of life and death without fear, and take pride in your bravery.

VALUES

Values are the bells that ring out the true notes of your character. They chime the principles of your life. They peal the essence of you to the world.

Your character is you at your best, your worst, and everything in between. You don't always expose your character by what you say or the things you claim you do. You reveal it by what you do when you think nobody is watching.

Which values do you claim to possess? List them out where you can see them. Itemize the ones you lack, but that you admire in others. Examples may include honesty, fairness, sincerity, respect, responsibility, and integrity. Don't forget self-discipline, courtesy, caring, compassion, service to others, and cheering people on to do well. Choose all those by which you would like to be known and remembered.

The fastest and most effective way to become the person you want to be is to write a moral and ethical code for yourself. Design the code to reflect the values you would like to guide your choices and directions in life. You can control your own character by incorporating those values into your thoughts and actions until they become habits.

You may be tempted to abandon your values when others board the bandwagons of popularity and acquiescence. Stand firm, though, and refuse to compromise your own high standards. If you exercise your strength and courage, you will foster your personal honor and pride.

You can assess other peoples' values by how they treat or speak of others, especially those they perceive as being somehow beneath them. Measure your own values by the behaviors you choose to condone or reject. The limits you set will define who you are.

Not everyone will see you as you see yourself. People will judge you by where you live and the friends you select. They may gossip and tarnish your reputation regardless of your actions or what lies in your heart. Only you will know your own truths.

Set high values. Live by them consistently so that you can always respect yourself.

50

WHOLENESS

You are your body, mind and spirit, but you are more than just their sum. You are the whole created by all your parts working together, just as the world is formed of its many interdependent components.

You may keep an eye on your checkbook and credit card balances, but how often do you look at the balance between the three essential portions of your life? Do you pay more attention to your physical appearance than the quality of your intellect? Are you more concerned with the health of your body than that of your emotions and soul?

Wholeness demands a reasonable balance among the dimensions that define you. Establishing and maintaining that balance requires you to look within yourself and evaluate what you see. Only you can know if a true balance exists within you, and only you can decide to correct an imbalance when it occurs.

You may be so caught up with the chores of daily living that you don't even notice when your dimensions get out of kilter. It is like frantically bailing a boat, but never taking time to fix the leak. Stop! Find and repair the holes in your life.

Wholeness implies integrity, and integrity means knowing and sticking to your values. Have you acted with sincerity, good sense and honor? How proud would you be if everyone in the world knew all the things you did? Or, better yet, if they knew the motives behind all the things you did?

Envision your integrity as a series of thermometers. Check the degrees of such things as your decency, morality and virtue. Note the levels you reach in keeping your promises and in the amount of good you do. Keep track of how you measure up on your concern for others and your ability to use power without abusing it.

See yourself in all living things. Be strong enough to stand against the opinion of the many when their opinion leads them down a path of wrongdoing.

Seek integrity. Be authentic. Become whole.

EXCELLENCE

Where do you rank on the excellence scale? Do you sing your heart out and strive to do the very best you can? Or do you spend your days sitting around and merely getting by?

Many of us slide toward a norm of mediocrity and do only what is expected of us. We justify our lack of effort by saying, "All I need is a passing grade," or "The pay's the same, whether I work hard or not." We even poke fun at people who work harder than we think they should, and demean their efforts by calling them workaholics.

Those who gain the greatest satisfaction and happiness from their accomplishments do so through excelling. Excelling does not imply achieving something to the exclusion of all else, nor should it be equated with perfection. A crusade for perfection may be a quest for excellence gone awry.

You can attain excellence through passion and persistence, even if raw talent and genius have passed you by. Excellence won't fall at your feet, however. You must pursue it with patience and effort through good times and bad, even when it tries to elude you. Make a habit of courting it every day.

Your positive attitude will energize you as you seek to excel. You must be willing to be your own master and demand more of yourself than others would ask of you. Only you will know if you have done your personal best. The satisfaction you gain from your personal efforts may eventually mean more to you than any rewards that others may confer.

Excellence applies to the accomplishment of ordinary tasks as well as to the extraordinary. No matter what you choose to do, try to do it well. People may not recollect exactly what you accomplished or the speed with which you did it, but they will always remember the quality of your work. Give them something excellent to recall.

Like the bird that sings, you have natural abilities. Excellence is a song wonderfully sung.

Persevere, and you will excel.

54

YOU

You. It's all up to you. It's about getting your inner tiger to take control and unleash the power of your own potential.

Don't make excuses or fall into the trap of inaction because you believe someone else is better than you. The tiger can't compete with the cheetah's speed, the lion's sociability or the leopard's tree-climbing prowess. Nevertheless, the world reveres it for its bold fierceness and patience before the pounce. Stop worrying about your shortcomings or how you compare with others. Find your niche and capitalize on the things you do the best.

You were born with talents and strengths that you probably never fully explored. Identify and nourish your gifts and powers. Problems or failures may slow you down, but hurdles exist to be jumped. Clearing them builds your confidence.

You can say "yes" to life as easily as you can say "no." Saying "yes" to the myriad bounties that life has to offer will bring you far more satisfaction and joy than bemoaning your fate and turning your back on fresh opportunities. Life is there for the taking. Grab on with both hands.

Stop wasting your energy fretting about all the things you haven't done, don't have, or think you will never do or get. If you had a dream that died, breathe life back into it. Disregard your failures and those who discourage you from trying. It is your life to live as you choose. Choose to live it well.

Use the power of your inner tiger to make a positive difference in this world. Refuse to tolerate bad behaviors, whether by individuals, businesses, organizations, religions, or governments. Insist on what is right and good. Don't just talk. Do.

If the grass looks greener on the other side of the fence, it probably is. That's because somebody fertilized, watered and mowed it. Greener grass or a better life doesn't just happen without effort. You have to know what you want and work to make it happen.

There is a tiger's potential within you, waiting and watching. Release its power now.

ZEST

Zest - *noun*
    1. hearty, spirited enjoyment; gusto
    2. intense enthusiasm rarely experienced by grownups

When was the last time that zest energized your life? Not just any ho-hum breed of enjoyment, but the true heart-pounding excitement that propels you out of bed, grinning, to start a new day or task? When did you last feel true passion for your work or activities? When was the last time you shouted your happiness to the world?

If zest is not a part of your everyday life, you are barely alive.

Zest is the new-fallen snow sparkling in the morning sun like a million diamonds, mist swirling up from a verdant valley on a spring morning, stars blinking above a mountain's inky crest, the sound of snow drifting down in a secluded forest, and the dazzling rainbow no artist's paint can ever capture. It is your first hayride, first love, the thrill of going to your first Broadway show, and the lusty cry of your new grandbaby. It is puppies or kittens clamoring over a child. It is unbridled optimism for the days to come. It is the thrill of applause when it's for you.

If you hold pity in your heart, hold it for those who have never known zest.

One of the best things about zest is that it need not cost you money. All it requires is a raging fire in your belly for the things that bring you joy. If you do not experience zest on a regular basis, perhaps you need to change the way you live or view your life.

Zest keeps you young. If your zest has waned, revitalize it with a fresh purpose. Pursue a different and exciting goal. Pour yourself into the quest and have fun.

Zest often comes calling when you create something new. Try it. The hidden talent and touch of genius you've harbored all along may just explode into a passion.

Embrace zest. Raise your head and shout your joy.

PHOTO SUBJECTS AND LOCATIONS

Attitude:	Ship's Doctor, M/V Grigoriy Mikheev, Deception Island, Antarctica
Believe:	Mourning Dove, Mt. Desert Island, Maine, USA
Choices:	Ostriches, Kenya, Africa
Dream:	Amazonian Girl, Rio Negro, Brazil, South America
Explore:	Aoraki/Mt. Cook, South Island, New Zealand
Forgive:	Bonnet Macaques, Maharashtra, India
Golden Rule:	Zebras, Kenya, Africa
Happiness:	Samburu Woman, Kenya, Africa
Invest:	Rainbow over Inner Bar Island, Corea, Maine, USA
Journey:	Country Road, Assam, India
Knowledge:	Spotted Owlet, Madhya Pradesh, India
Love:	Hippopotamuses, Tanzania, Africa
Motivation:	Crew Member, M/V Grigoriy Mikheev, Petermann Island, Antarctica
Nature:	Waterfall, Lakes Region, Southern Chile, South America
Opportunity:	Visitor, Schoodic Point, Winter Harbor, Maine, USA
Play:	Dancers, Virungo Volcanoes Region, Rwanda, Africa
Question:	Rhesus Macaque, Swayambhunath, Kathmandu, Nepal
Responsibility:	Elephants, Tanzania, Africa
Smile:	Rock Hyrax, Olduvai Gorge, Tanzania, Africa
Time:	Phyllis Silverman at age 97, Corea, Maine, USA
Unknown:	Sailing Under the Southern Cross, East Coast of South America
Values:	Child and Temple Bell, Pokhara, Nepal
Wholeness:	Setting Sun, Chitwan District, Nepal
e**X**cellence:	Chestnut-Headed Bee Eater, Narayani River, Nepal
You:	Royal Bengal Tiger, Madhya Pradesh, India
Zest:	Chinstrap Penguins, Ardley Island, Antarctica

All photos © 2013 by Beth Parks, Ed.D.

Photos and photo gift items may be purchased through www.bethparksphoto.com
Photos from this book appear in the "A Is for Attitude" gallery.

ABOUT THE AUTHOR

Dr. Beth Parks is a writer and photographer whose works have appeared in newspapers and magazines, as well as on national television. She travels extensively and has visited all seven continents, dozens of countries and all fifty United States.

Beth enjoyed successful careers as a Cooperative Extension educator and professor, wildlife biologist, researcher, and public information specialist. She was also a registered nurse who served in operating rooms in MASH and evacuation hospitals in Vietnam.

In writing *A Is for Attitude*, Beth drew heavily from her life-threatening bout with cancer, the deaths of three dear ones within a few months, and a near-fatal car accident.

Beth also produced a powerful film called *A Chunk of My Soul*, which combines her still photographs with live-action footage to help viewers understand the nurses' experience in the Vietnam War. She is pleased to show the film in educational settings.

Learn more about Beth and her projects at bethparks.com, bethparksphoto.com, schoodicstudio.com, and sibylmerritt.com.

COMING SOOM FROM BETH PARKS

SIBYL MERRITT™
PUBLISHER

A young cow falls in love with a whale in this rhyming fantasy set in Maine's Acadia National Park. The Keeper of the Sea angrily disapproves of the match. What does he do when the cow disobeys him, and the cow and whale produce a son?

Danielle Armitage Demers' delightful illustrations breathe life into the story and help readers learn about the Acadia region and Maine's navigational buoys. The book's short glossary helps young readers and listeners build their vocabularies.

The Sea Cow
A Rhyming Tale Set in Acadia National Park

Beth Parks, Ed.D.
Illustrated by Danielle Armitage Demers

A Rhyming Tale Set in Borneo

A young proboscis monkey worries because his nose is smaller than the ones of other males. When the others tease and bully him, he pulls and stretches and tugs on his nose to make it bigger. And then something happens...

Winning by a Nose

Beth Parks, Ed.D.

How miserable are you when you catch a cold? An elephant seal pup in Antarctica snags a bad one. The cold spreads through the seal colony much as it would through a family or classroom.

The first portion of ELEPHANT SEALS WITH COLDS IN THEIR NOSES is a rhyming fantasy tale for children and those who like to read to them.

The book's second portion provides photos and facts to help children and adults learn about southern elephant seals.

Elephant Seals with Colds In Their Noses
FANTASY & FACT IN ANTARCTICA

BETH PARKS, ED.D.

Morris, a young male Adelie penguin in Antarctica, returns to his traditional rookery to mate and raise a family. He sadly discovers that a colony of Gentoo penguins has moved in and taken over the nesting site that his family has used for generations.

Adelie penguins must have a colder climate than Gentoos to survive. Morris realizes that the weather has become too hot for Adelies. He and his girlfriend must head south and search for a chillier place to nest and raise their chicks.

Too Hot for Penguins
A Rhyming Tale Set in Antarctica

Beth Parks, Ed.D.

Hurricane Bill was only the third hurricane, after Hurricane Gloria in 1985 and Hurricane Bob in 1999, to threaten the coast of Maine in 50 years.

As with most hurricane-level storms bound for Maine, Bill lost much of its power as it moved northward over the cold Atlantic waters.

The "old sea" left behind by Hurricane Bill produced spectacular surf in Corea, Maine. Although onlookers generally remained safe, a rogue wave washed more than a dozen spectators into the sea at nearby Acadia National Park. A 7-year-old girl drowned.

The photos in this book showcase Corea's surf on the afternoon of August 23, 2009.

Hurricane Bill

Beth Parks, Ed.D.

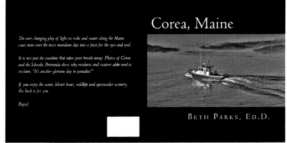

The ever-changing play of light on rocks and water along the Maine coast turns even the most mundane day into a feast for the eyes and soul.

It is not just the coastline that takes your breath away. Photos of Corea and the Schoodic Peninsula show why residents and visitors alike tend to exclaim, "It's another glorious day in paradise!"

If you enjoy the ocean, lobster boats, wildlife and spectacular scenery, this book is for you.

Enjoy!

Corea, Maine

BETH PARKS, ED.D.

60

Proof

Made in the USA
Charleston, SC
18 January 2013